PROSECCO

CLASSIC &
CONTEMPORARY
COCKTAILS

An Hachette UK Company
www.hachette.co.uk

First published in Great Britain in 2018 by Hamlyn,
an imprint of Octopus Publishing Group Ltd
Carmelite House, 50 Victoria Embankment, London EC4Y 0DZ
www.octopusbooks.co.uk

ISBN 978-0-75373-309-7

A CIP catalogue record for this book is available from the British Library

Printed and bound in China

10 9 8 7 6 5 4 3 2

Publisher: Lucy Pessell
Designer: Lisa Layton
Editor: Sarah Vaughan
Production Controller: Dasha Miller
Cover and interior motifs created by: Abhimanyu Bose, LSE Designs, Magicon,
Valeriy, Wuppdidu. All from *The Noun Project.*

The measure that has been used in the recipes is based on a bar jigger, which is 25 ml (1 fl oz).
If preferred, a different volume can be used, providing the proportions are kept constant within a
drink and suitable adjustments are made to spoon measurements, where they occur.

Standard level spoon measurements are used in all recipes.
1 tablespoon = one 15 ml spoon
1 teaspoon = one 5 ml spoon

This book contains cocktails made with raw or lightly cooked eggs. It is prudent for more vulnerable
people to avoid uncooked or lightly cooked cocktails made with eggs.

Some of this material previously appeared in *Hamlyn All Colour Cookery: 200 Classic Cocktails* and
501 Must-Drink Cocktails.

PROSECCO

CLASSIC &
CONTEMPORARY
COCKTAILS

hamlyn

CONTENTS

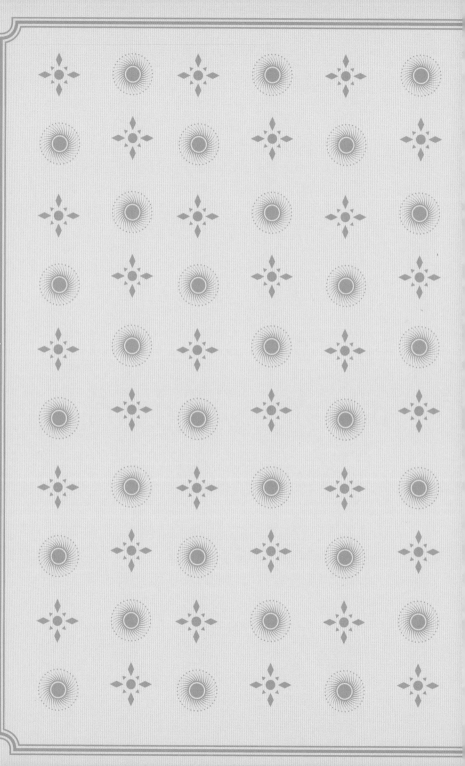

A BRIEF HISTORY OF PROSECCO & COCKTAILS

The origin of the word '𝒞𝒪𝒞𝒦𝒯𝒜ℐℒ' is widely disputed.

Initially used to describe the docked tails of horses that were not thoroughbred (which hasn't much to do with a Singapore Sling), the alleged first definition of a 'cocktail' appeared in New York's *The Balance and Columbian Repository*. In response to the question 'What is a cocktail?' the editor replied: 'it is a stimulating liquor, composed of spirits of any kind, sugar, water and bitters... in as much as it renders the heart stout and bold, at the same time that it fuddles the head... because a person, having swallowed a glass of it, is ready to swallow anything else'. Which sounds a little more like it.

However it began, this delightful act of mixing varying amounts of spirits, sugar and bitters has evolved, after decades of fine crafting, experimentation and even 13 years of prohibition in the United States, into the 'cocktail' we know and love. Each one a masterpiece. Each one to be made just right for you.

In the century since Harry Craddock concocted the Corpse Reviver and the White Lady, James Bond has insisted on breaking the number 1 rule to not shake a Martini every time he goes to the bar, and *Sex and the City* has introduced a whole new generation of drinkers to the very pink, very fabulous, Cosmopolitan cocktail. And the idea it can be paired with a burger and fries. Which is fine by us.

Go forth and make yours a Martini. Or a French Afternoon at gin o'clock on a mizzly Monday morning.

PROSECCO is an Italian sparkling (spumante) or semi-sparkling (frizzante) white wine.

Originally made with the 'Glera' grape, and hailing from the Italian village of Prosecco near Trieste, Prosecco as we know it is now produced in nine provinces, and often from a blend of grapes. It has officially been recognised as 'the best thing ever' and has been protected by DOC and DOCG status.

Its popularity in the last decade has rocketed and the idea that Prosecco is simply Champagne's poor cousin is on the wane. Prosecco, with its light and spritzy bubbles is often fruitier and more floral than Champagne, and just happens to be cheaper as its aging time is a fraction of that of Champagne's: tank-aged rather than bottle-aged.

Prosecco is at the effervescent heart of the Bellini, and is the magic ingredient in the Italian Spritz recipe but it has a place in every cocktail that calls for bubbles.

Here we've collected 100 recipes – some classic 'Champagne' cocktails dating back to times before we'd even heard of Prosecco (imagine! The Dark Ages!), some modern twists and some 'skip the soda and bring on the bubbles' creations.

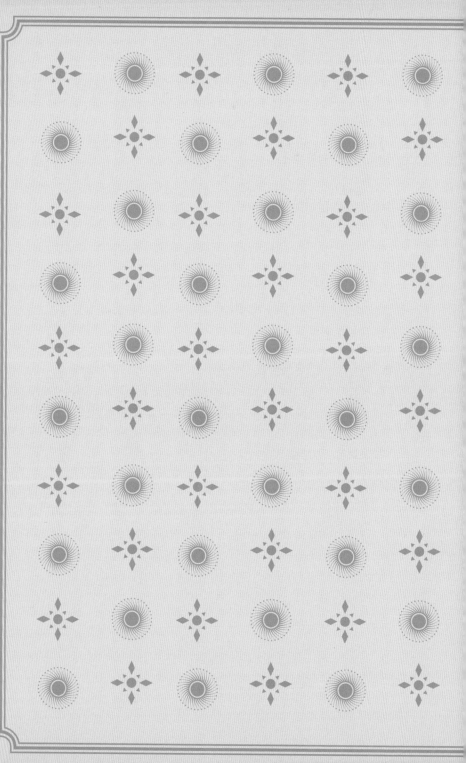

LIGHT & FLORAL

NEW DAWN COOLER

1 MEASURE VODKA

2 MEASURES APPLE JUICE

½ MEASURE PASSION FRUIT SYRUP

PROSECCO, TO TOP

GRAPES, TO GARNISH

Add all the ingredients except the Prosecco to a highball glass filled with cubed ice.

Stir well, top with chilled Prosecco and garnish with white grapes.

ORCHARD BELLINI

½ RIPE WHITE PEACH

1 MEASURE APPLE JUICE

DASH OF SUGAR SYRUP

PROSECCO, TO TOP

Add the peach and sugar syrup to a blender or food processor and blend until smooth.

Pour into a Champagne flute with the apple juice and the sugar syrup and top with chilled Prosecco.

CHESHIRE CAT

1 MEASURE VODKA

1 MEASURE DRY VERMOUTH

1 MEASURE ORANGE JUICE

PROSECCO, TO TOP

ORANGE, TO GARNISH

Add all of the ingredients except the Prosecco to a rocks glass filled with cubed ice and stir briefly.

Top with chilled Prosecco and garnish with an orange wedge.

COBBLER FIZZ

1 MEASURE FINO SHERRY

3 RASPBERRIES

1 MEASURE ORANGE JUICE

PROSECCO, TO TOP

RASPBERRIES, TO GARNISH

Add the sherry, orange juice and raspberries to your cocktail shaker and shake well.

Strain into a Champagne flute and top with chilled Prosecco.

Garnish with a raspberry.

FLORAL BELLINI

½ MEASURE ROSE LIQUEUR

1 TSP LAVENDER SYRUP

2 MEASURES GRAPEFRUIT JUICE

PROSECCO, TO TOP

DRIED LAVENDER FLOWERS, TO GARNISH

Pour the rose liqueur, lavender syrup and grapefruit juice into a cocktail shaker or mixing glass filled with cubed ice.

Stir for 10 seconds and strain into a Champagne flute.

Top with chilled Prosecco and garnish with dried lavender flowers.

SAKURA PUNCH

1 MEASURE VODKA

1 MEASURE LYCHEE JUICE

1 MEASURE GRAPEFRUIT JUICE

2 TSP ROSE SYRUP

PROSECCO, TO TOP

GRAPEFRUIT & COCKTAIL CHERRY, TO GARNISH

Add all the ingredients except the Prosecco to a rocks glass filled with cubed ice, stir well and top with chilled Prosecco.

Garnish with a slice of grapefruit and a cocktail cherry.

PRIMROSE FIZZ

½ MEASURE ELDERFLOWER CORDIAL

1 MEASURE APPLE JUICE

6 MINT LEAVES

PROSECCO, TO TOP

APPLE, TO GARNISH

Squeeze the mint leaves in your hand to express the oils, then drop them into a wine glass.

Add the elderflower cordial and apple juice, fill with cubed ice and top with chilled Prosecco.

Stir briefly and garnish with apple slices.

CICLOMOTORE

2 MEASURES APEROL

PROSECCO, TO TOP

ORANGE, TO GARNISH

Pour the Aperol into a rocks glass filled with cubed ice.

Top with chilled Prosecco and garnish with a slice of orange.

LYCHEE & APEROL

2 MEASURES APEROL

2 MEASURES LYCHEE JUICE

PROSECCO, TO TOP

ORANGE, TO GARNISH

Add the Aperol and lychee juice to a wine glass filled with cubed ice.

Stir well, top with chilled Prosecco and garnish with a slice of orange.

23

ZAN LA CAY

½ MEASURE CRÈME DE PECHE

1 TSP LEMON JUICE

2 CUBES CUCUMBER

1 GREEN CARDAMOM POD

PROSECCO, TO TOP

CUCUMBER, TO GARNISH

Muddle the cucumber and
cardamom in a cocktail shaker
and then add all the ingredients
except the Prosecco.

Shake well and strain into a
Champagne flute.

Top with chilled Prosecco and
garnish with a slice of cucumber.

25

FRENCH AFTERNOON

1 MEASURE GIN

½ MEASURE LEMON JUICE

1 MEASURE CAMOMILE TEA, CHILLED

¾ MEASURE SUGAR SYRUP

PROSECCO, TO TOP

LEMON, TO GARNISH

Add all the ingredients except the Prosecco to you cocktail shaker, shake well and strain into a highball glass.

Top with chilled Prosecco and garnish with a lemon twist.

COTTER KIR

2 TSP CRÈME DE CASSIS

2 TSP RASPBERRY LIQUEUR

1 MEASURE CRANBERRY JUICE

PROSECCO, TO TOP

RASPBERRIES, TO GARNISH

Add all the ingredients except the Prosecco to a wine glass filled with cubed ice and stir briefly.

Top with chilled Prosecco and garnish with raspberries.

CUCUMBER RANGOON

1 MEASURE PIMM'S NO.1 CUP

2 MEASURES CUCUMBER JUICE

2 TSP GINGER JUICE

2 TSP SUGAR SYRUP

PROSECCO, TO TOP

CUCUMBER, TO GARNISH

Add all the ingredients to a wine glass filled with cubed ice.

Top with chilled Prosecco and garnish with a slice of cucumber.

28

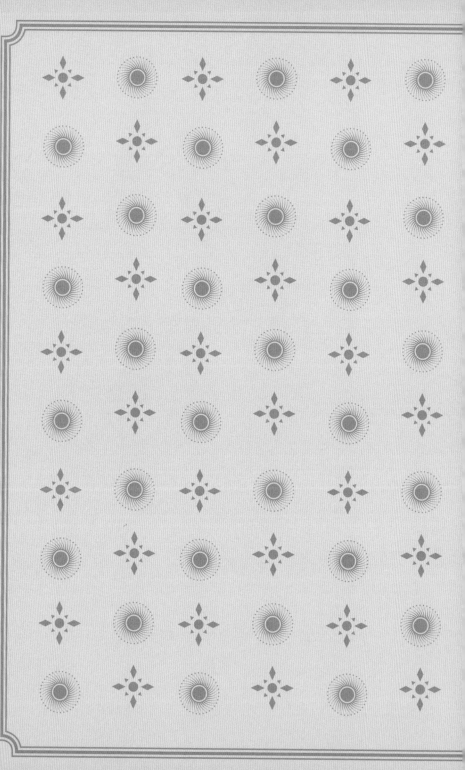

VIBRANT & ZESTY

BITTER SPRING
SPRITZ

1 MEASURE APEROL

2 MEASURES GRAPEFRUIT JUICE

PROSECCO, TO TOP

GRAPEFRUIT, TO GARNISH

Add the Aperol and grapefruit juice
to a rocks glass filled with cubed ice.

Stir briefly, top with chilled Prosecco
and garnish with a grapefruit wedge.

ROYAL COBBLER

1 MEASURE GIN

½ MEASURE RASPBERRY SYRUP

½ MEASURE LEMON JUICE

1 MEASURE PINEAPPLE JUICE

PROSECCO, TO TOP

RASPBERRIES, TO GARNISH

Add all the ingredients except the Prosecco to a cocktail shaker and shake well.

Strain into a rocks glass filled with cubed ice and top with chilled Prosecco.

Garnish with raspberries.

SUNSHINE STATE

1 MEASURE GIN

½ MEASURE ELDERFLOWER LIQUEUR

2 TSP LEMON JUICE

1 MEASURE APPLE JUICE

6 MINT LEAVES

PROSECCO, TO TOP

STRAWBERRY, TO GARNISH

Squeeze the mint leaves in your hand to express the oils, then drop them into a highball glass.

Add the gin, elderflower liqueur, lemon juice and apple juice, fill with cubed ice and top with chilled Prosecco.

Stir briefly and garnish with slices of strawberry.

MANDARIN 75

1 MEASURE COINTREAU

½ MEASURE LEMON JUICE

2 TSP SUGAR SYRUP

PROSECCO, TO TOP

ORANGE, TO GARNISH

Add the Cointreau, lemon juice and sugar syrup to a chilled Champagne flute.

Top with chilled Prosecco and garnish with an orange twist.

37

LOS ALTOS

2 MEASURES TEQUILA

½ MEASURE LIME JUICE

2 MEASURES ORANGE JUICE

3 TSP AGAVE SYRUP

2 TSP CAMPARI

PROSECCO, TO TOP

ORANGE & LIME, TO GARNISH

Add all the ingredients except the Prosecco to your cocktail shaker, shake and strain into a hurricane glass filled with cubed ice.

Top with chilled Prosecco and garnish with a lime wedge and a slice of orange.

TANKA COBBLER

1 MEASURE FINO SHERRY

½ MEASURE LEMON JUICE

2 TSP SUGAR SYRUP

4 RASPBERRIES

PROSECCO, TO TOP

RASPBERRIES, TO GARNISH

Add the Fino Sherry, lemon juice, sugar syrup and raspberries to your cocktail shaker.

Shake well and strain into to highball glass filled with crushed ice.

Top with chilled Prosecco and more crushed ice and garnish with raspberries.

GOLDEN APRICOT

1 MEASURE RUM

½ MEASURE APRICOT LIQUEUR

½ MEASURE LIME JUICE

2 TSP SUGAR SYRUP

PROSECCO, TO TOP

LIME, TO GARNISH

Add all ingredients to a highball glass filled with cubed ice and stir well.

Top with chilled Prosecco and garnish with a lime wedge.

SPANISH HARLEM

1 MEASURE FINO SHERRY

1 MEASURE ORANGE JUICE

PROSECCO, TO TOP

Add the Fino sherry and orange
juice to a Champagne flute and top
with chilled Prosecco.

PEACHES & GREEN

1 MEASURE VODKA

1 MEASURE GREEN TEA, CHILLED

½ RIPE WHITE PEACH

1 TSP LEMON JUICE

1 DASH SUGAR SYRUP

PROSECCO, TO TOP

Add all the ingredients except the Prosecco to a blender or food processor and blend until smooth.

Pour into a wine glass filled with cubed ice and top with chilled Prosecco.

43

HONEY DEW

1 MEASURE GIN

½ MEASURE LEMON JUICE

½ MEASURE SUGAR SYRUP

2 DROPS ABSINTHE (OR PERNOD)

5 CUBES HONEYDEW MELON

PROSECCO, TO TOP

LEMON & ROSEMARY, TO GARNISH

Add all the ingredients except the Prosecco to a blender or food processor and blend with 5 cubes of ice.

Pour into a chilled wine glass, top with chilled Prosecco and garnish with a lemon twist and a sprig of rosemary.

PASSIONFRUIT SPRITZ

1 MEASURE VANILLA VODKA

1 MEASURE PASSION FRUIT SYRUP

½ MEASURE LEMON JUICE

PROSECCO, TO TOP

MINT & PASSIONFRUIT, TO GARNISH

Add the vodka, passion fruit syrup and lemon juice to a wine glass filled with cubed ice.

Stir well, top with chilled Prosecco and garnish with half a passion fruit and a sprig of mint.

CHAIN REACTION

1 MEASURE VODKA

1 MEASURE LEMON JUICE

2 TSP SUGAR SYRUP

PROSECCO, TO TOP

LEMON, TO GARNISH

Add the vodka, lemon juice and sugar syrup to your cocktail shaker, shake and strain into a Champagne flute and top with chilled Prosecco.

Garnish with a twist of lemon.

47

AMBIKA BELLINI

4 SLICES MANGO

2 TSP GRENADINE

PROSECCO, TO TOP

Add the mango and grenadine to a blender or food processor and blend until smooth.

Pour into a Champagne flute and top with chilled Prosecco.

MONTECARLO SLING

1 MEASURE COGNAC

1 MEASURE PEACH LIQUEUR

1 MEASURE ORANGE JUICE

PROSECCO, TO TOP

ORANGE, TO GARNISH

Pour the cognac, peach liqueur and orange juice into a highball glass filled with cubed ice.

Top with chilled Prosecco and garnish with a slice of orange.

NEHRU

1 MEASURE GIN

4 SLICES FRESH MANGO

5 PINK PEPPERCORNS

PROSECCO, TO TOP

Add the gin, mango and peppercorns to a blender or food processor and blend until smooth.

Strain into a Champagne flute and top with chilled Prosecco.

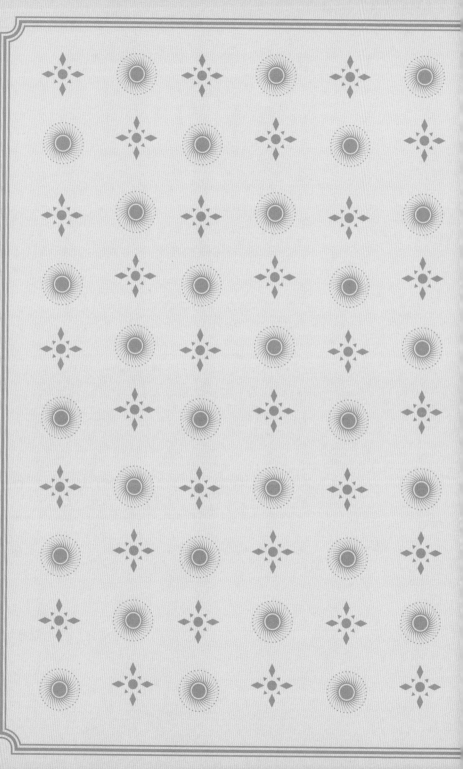

INTENSE
& SULTRY

SPICE ROUTE PUNCH

1 MEASURE CINNAMON-INFUSED COGNAC

(SEE PAGE 115)

½ MEASURE LEMON JUICE

½ MEASURE SUGAR SYRUP

2 MEASURES GINGER ALE

PROSECCO, TO TOP

CINNAMON STICK & APPLE, TO GARNISH

In a glass, combine 1 measure
cognac with 1 tsp of cinnamon and
leave for 10 minutes (see page 115 for
a more intense version).

Strain the cognac into a wine glass
filled with cubed ice, and add the
lemon juice, sugar syrup and
ginger ale.

Top with chilled Prosecco, stir, and
garnish with a cinnamon stick and
slices of apple.

DEVIL'S ADVOCATE

½ MEASURE CAMPARI

1 MEASURE BLOOD ORANGE JUICE

½ MEASURE SUGAR SYRUP

PROSECCO, TO TOP

ORANGE, TO GARNISH

Add the cognac, Cointreau and sugar syrup into a cocktail shaker or mixing glass filled with cubed ice.

Stir for 10 seconds and strain into a Champagne flute.

Top with chilled Prosecco and garnish with a twist of orange.

PINK SANGRIA

2 MEASURES ROSÉ WINE

1 ½ MEASURES POMEGRANATE JUICE

2 TSP AGAVE SYRUP

PROSECCO, TO TOP

PINK GRAPEFRUIT, TO GARNISH

Add all ingredients except the Prosecco to a wine glass filled with cubed ice.

Stir briefly, top with chilled Prosecco and garnish with a slice of pink grapefruit.

RUBY TUESDAY

1 MEASURE RUM

½ MEASURE LIME JUICE

½ MEASURE SUGAR SYRUP

6 RASPBERRIES

PROSECCO, TO TOP

RASPBERRY, TO GARNISH

Add the rum, lime juice, sugar syrup and raspberries to a blender or food processor and blend until smooth.

Pour into a Champagne flute and top with chilled Prosecco.

Garnish with a raspberry.

BUBBLE BERRY

½ MEASURE RASPBERRY LIQUEUR

½ MEASURE BLACKBERRY LIQUEUR

PROSECCO, TO TOP

RASPBERRY & BLACKBERRY, TO GARNISH

Add the liqueurs to a Champagne flute and top with chilled Prosecco.

Drop in a raspberry and a blackberry to garnish.

59

CHAMPINO

1 MEASURE CAMPARI

1 MEASURE SWEET VERMOUTH

PROSECCO, TO TOP

LEMON, TO GARNISH

Add the Campari and sweet vermouth to a Champagne flute.

Top with chilled Prosecco and garnish with a lemon twist.

MELON SPRITZ

1 MEASURE MELON LIQUEUR

½ MEASURE APEROL

2 MEASURES SODA WATER

PROSECCO, TO TOP

MINT, TO GARNISH

Add the melon liqueur, aperol and soda water to a wine glass filled with cubed ice.

Top with chilled Prosecco and garnish with a mint sprig.

61

BLACKWOOD BLUSH

2 MEASURES GRAPEFRUIT JUICE

2 MEASURES ROSÉ WINE

2 TSP CRÈME DE MURE

PROSECCO, TO TOP

GRAPEFRUIT & THYME, TO GARNISH

Add all ingredients except the Prosecco to a wine glass filled with cubed ice.

Top with chilled Prosecco, stir well and garnish with a slice of grapefruit and a sprig of thyme.

NEVER FORGOTTEN LISA

½ MEASURE SLOE GIN

½ MEASURE STRAWBERRY LIQUEUR

2 TSP LEMON JUICE

PROSECCO, TO TOP

STRAWBERRY, TO GARNISH

Add the gin, strawberry liqueur and lemon juice to your cocktail shaker, shake and strain into a Champagne flute.

Top with chilled Prosecco.

Garnish with a strawberry.

CELEBRATION COCKTAIL

1 MEASURE COGNAC

1 TSP CRÈME DE MURE

1 TSP BENEDICTINE

1 LEMON WEDGE

CASTER SUGAR

PROSECCO, TO TOP

Frost the rim of a Champagne flute by moistening it with the lemon wedge and dipping it in the caster sugar.

Add the Cognac, Crème de Mure and Benedictine to the glass and top with chilled Prosecco.

G & TEA SPRITZ

½ MEASURE STRAWBERRY LIQUEUR

1 TSP LEMON JUICE

1 TSP SUGAR SYRUP

2 MEASURES EARL GREY TEA, CHILLED

PROSECCO, TO TOP

MINT, TO GARNISH

Add all the ingredients except the Prosecco to a wine glass filled with cubed ice.

Top with chilled Prosecco and garnish with a mint sprig.

FRENCH MARTINI

½ MEASURE VODKA

½ MEASURE CHAMBORD

1 MEASURE PINEAPPLE JUICE

PROSECCO, TO TOP

MINT, TO GARNISH

Add the vodka, Chambord and pineapple juice to your cocktail shaker, shake well and strain into a chilled cocktail glass.

Top with chilled Prosecco.

Garnish with a mint leaf.

67

LA ROCHELLE PUNCH

1 MEASURE COGNAC

1 MEASURE CHAMBORD

½ MEASURE LEMON JUICE

½ MEASURE SUGAR SYRUP

PROSECCO, TO TOP

RASPBERRIES & BLACKBERRIES, TO GARNISH

Add the cognac, Chambord, lemon juice and sugar syrup to a rocks glass filled with cubed ice.

Stir well, top with chilled Prosecco and garnish with raspberries and blackberries.

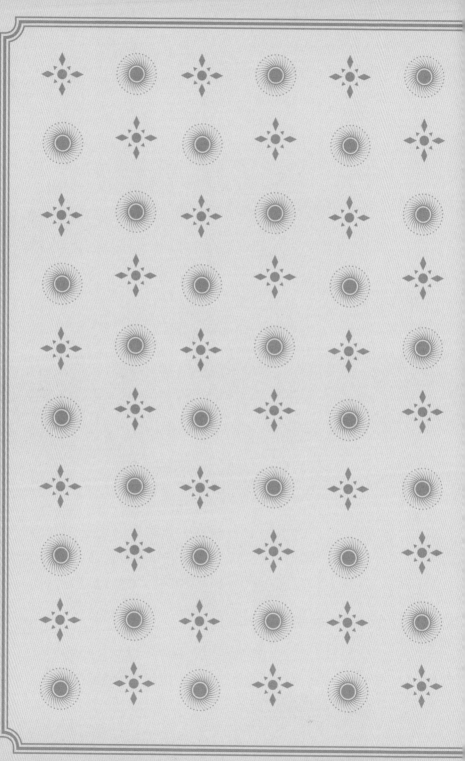

SHARERS &
PUNCHES

LOLA'S PUNCH

3 MEASURES WHITE RUM

3 MEASURES LEMON JUICE

3 MEASURES APPLE JUICE

3 MEASURES MANGO JUICE

3 MEASURES SUGAR SYRUP

4 MEASURES SODA WATER

PROSECCO, TO TOP

MANGO & APPLE, TO GARNISH

Add all the ingredients to a jug or punch bowl filled with cubed ice and stir well.

Garnish with slices of mango and apple.

HEDGEROW PUNCH

3 MEASURES SLOE GIN

1 MEASURE CRÈME DE CASSIS

2 MEASURES LEMON JUICE

2 MEASURES GRAPEFRUIT JUICE

2 MEASURES SUGAR SYRUP

PROSECCO, TO TOP

BLACKBERRIES & MINT, TO GARNISH

Add all the ingredients to a jug or punch bowl filled with cubed ice and stir well.

Garnish with blackberries and sprigs of mint.

ISAMBARD'S PUNCH

4 MEASURES GIN

2 MEASURES CHERRY BRANDY

1 MEASURE CAMPARI

4 MEASURES POMEGRANATE JUICE

4 MEASURES GRAPEFRUIT JUICE

2 MEASURES SUGAR SYRUP

PROSECCO, TO TOP

MINT & GRAPEFRUIT, TO GARNISH

Add all the ingredients to a jug or punch bowl filled with cubed ice and stir well.

Garnish with grapefruit slices and sprigs of mint.

BLUSH SANGRIA

4 MEASURES VODKA

2 MEASURES RASPBERRY LIQUEUR

4 MEASURES CRANBERRY JUICE

2 MEASURES LIME JUICE

1 MEASURE SUGAR SYRUP

PROSECCO, TO TOP

EDIBLE FLOWERS, TO GARNISH

Add all the ingredients to a jug or punch bowl filled with cubed ice and stir well.

Garnish with edible flowers.

PARISIAN FIZZ

2 MEASURES RASPBERRY PUREE

4 MEASURES PASSION FRUIT JUICE

2 MEASURES SUGAR SYRUP

1 MEASURE PERNOD

1 BOTTLE PROSECCO

RASPBERRIES & MINT, TO GARNISH

Add all the ingredients to a punch bowl filled with cubed ice and stir well.

Garnish with raspberries and sprigs of mint.

WHITE SANGRIA

4 MEASURES VODKA

6 MEASURES APPLE JUICE

2 MEASURES LEMON JUICE

2 MEASURES ELDERFLOWER CORDIAL

4 MEASURES SODA WATER

PROSECCO, TO TOP

APPLE, LEMON & MINT, TO GARNISH

Add of the ingredients to a jug filled with cubed ice and stir well.

Garnish with apple and lemon slices, and sprigs of mint.

79

WATERMELON PUNCH

3 MEASURES VODKA

1 MEASURE STRAWBERRY LIQUEUR

8 MEASURES WATERMELON JUICE

2 MEASURES LIME JUICE

2 MEASURES SUGAR SYRUP

1 X HANDFUL TORN MINT LEAVES

PROSECCO, TO TOP

WATERMELON, MINT & STRAWBERRY, TO GARNISH

Add all the ingredients to a jug or punch bowl filled with cubed ice and stir well.

Garnish with slices of watermelon, whole strawberries and sprigs of mint.

VESPERTILLO

4 MEASURES APEROL

4 PINKS PINK GRAPEFRUIT

2 MEASURES PASSION FRUIT SYRUP

1 MEASURE LEMON JUICE

PROSECCO, TO TOP

ORANGE & GRAPEFRUIT, TO GARNISH

Add all the ingredients to a jug or punch bowl filled with cubed ice and stir well.

Garnish with slices of orange and grapefruit.

CARMELITE DORIS

6 MEASURES RUM

1 MEASURE CAMPARI

2 MEASURES PASSIONFRUIT SYRUP

2 MEASURES LEMON JUICE

6 MEASURES PINEAPPLE JUICE

PROSECCO, TO TOP

LEMON & MINT, TO GARNISH

Add all the ingredients to a jug or punch bowl filled with cubed ice and stir well.

Garnish with slices lemon and sprigs of mint.

BLUEGRASS PUNCH

4 MEASURES BOURBON

3 TSP ORANGE MARMALADE

2 MEASURES LEMON JUICE

1 MEASURE SUGAR SYRUP

4 MEASURES SODA WATER

PROSECCO, TO TOP

ORANGE, TO GARNISH

Add all the ingredients to a jug or punch bowl filled with cubed ice and stir well.

Garnish with orange wheel slices.

FISH HOUSE PUNCH

1 MEASURE COGNAC

1 MEASURE RUM

½ PEACH LIQUEUR

1 MEASURE LEMON JUICE

½ MEASURE SUGAR SYRUP

PROSECCO, TO TOP

LEMON, TO GARNISH

Add all ingredients except the Prosecco to your cocktail shaker and shake vigorously.

Strain into a wine glass filled with cubed ice, top with chilled Prosecco and garnish with a lemon wedge.

TIPSY THERESE

1 MEASURE GIN

1 MEASURE WHITE RUM

1 MEASURE COGNAC

1 MEASURE DRY SHERRY

1 MEASURE SUGAR SYRUP

4 MEASURES ORANGE JUICE

PROSECCO, TO TOP

COCKTAIL CHERRIES, ORANGE & MINT, TO GARNISH

Add all the ingredients to a jug or punch bowl filled with cubed ice and stir well.

Garnish with cocktail cherries, orange slices and sprigs of mint.

87

TINTO VENEZIA

4 MEASURES APEROL

4 MEASURES PINK GRAPEFRUIT JUICE

4 MEASURES ORANGE JUICE

4 MEASURES ROSÉ WINE

PROSECCO, TO TOP

ORANGE & GRAPEFRUIT, TO GARNISH

Add the Aperol, grapefruit juice, orange juice and rosé wine to a large jug filed with cubed ice.

Stir well and top with chilled Prosecco.

Garnish with slices of orange and grapefruit.

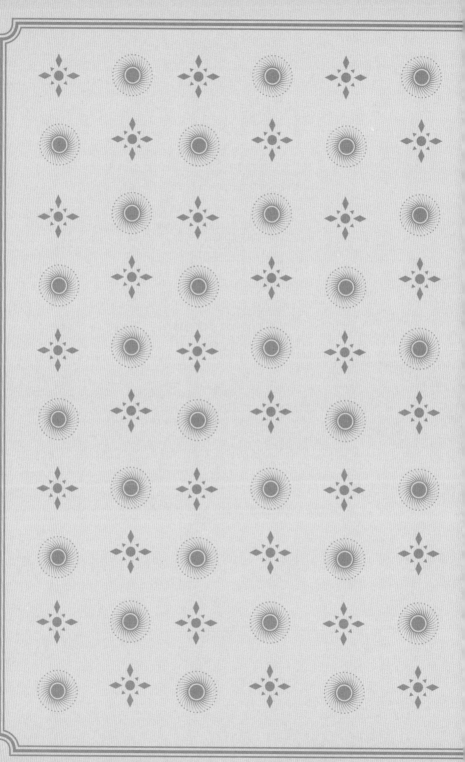

BELLINI

½ RIPE WHITE PEACH

1 DASH SUGAR SYRUP

PROSECCO, TO TOP

Add the peach and sugar syrup to a blender or food processor and blend until smooth.

Pour into a Champagne flute and top with chilled Prosecco.

GORGEOUS GRACE

1 MEASURE COGNAC

½ MEASURE COINTREAU

1 TSP SUGAR SYRUP

PROSECCO, TO TOP

ORANGE, TO GARNISH

Add the cognac, Cointreau and sugar syrup into a cocktail shaker or mixing glass filled with cubed ice.

Stir for 10 seconds and strain into a Champagne flute.

Top with chilled Prosecco and garnish with a twist of orange.

AIRMAIL

1 MEASURE WHITE RUM

½ MEASURE LIME JUICE

1 TSP HONEY

PROSECCO, TO TOP

Add the rum, lime juice and honey to your cocktail shaker and shake well.

Strain into a chilled cocktail glass and top with chilled Prosecco.

SOUTHSIDE ROYALE

1 ½ MEASURES GIN

¾ MEASURE LIME JUICE

¾ MEASURE SUGAR SYRUP

6 MINT LEAVES

PROSECCO, TO TOP

MINT, TO GARNISH

Add all the ingredients except the Prosecco to your cocktail shaker, shake vigorously and double strain into a chilled cocktail glass.

Top with chilled Prosecco and garnish with a mint leaf.

THE CLASSIC'S CLASSIC

1 MEASURE GRAND MARNIER

1 SUGAR CUBE

3-4 DASHES ANGOSTURA BITTERS

PROSECCO, TO TOP

LEMON, TO FINISH

On a clean surface, coat the sugar cube in the Angostura bitters then drop it into a Champagne flute.

Add the Grand Marnier and gently top with chilled Prosecco.

To finish, spray the oils of a lemon twist over the top of the drink, then discard it.

97

KIR ROYALE

1 MEASURE CRÈME DE CASSIS

PROSECCO, TO TOP

Pour the Crème de Cassis into
a Champagne flute and top
with chilled Prosecco.

MOJITO ROYALE

1 ½ MEASURES WHITE RUM

8 LIME WEDGES

2 TSP CASTER SUGAR

8 MINT LEAVES

PROSECCO, TO TOP

MINT, TO GARNISH

Muddle the mint, sugar and limes in a highball glass, add the rum and stir well.

Fill the glass with crushed ice, and churn vigorously.

Top with more crushed ice and chilled Prosecco, and garnish with a mint sprig.

FRESH PALOMA

1 MEASURE TEQUILA

2 TSP AGAVE SYRUP

2 MEASURES FRESH GRAPEFRUIT JUICE

PROSECCO, TO TOP

GRAPEFRUIT, TO GARNISH

Add all the ingredients to a highball glass filled with cubed ice, stir well and garnish with a slice of grapefruit.

ITALIAN DANDY

1 MEASURE COGNAC

1 TSP CHERRY BRANDY

1 TSP SUGAR SYRUP

PROSECCO, TO TOP

LEMON, TO GARNISH

Pour the cognac, cherry brandy and sugar syrup into a cocktail shaker or mixing glass filled with cubed ice.

Stir for 10 seconds and strain into a Champagne flute.

Top with chilled Prosecco and garnish with a twist of lemon.

BUCK'S FIZZ

2 MEASURES CHILLED FRESH ORANGE JUICE

4 MEASURES PROSECCO

Add half the Prosecco, chilled, to a Champagne flute, then carefully add the orange juice and the rest of the Prosecco.

103

PROSECCO JULEP

1 MEASURE COGNAC

8 MINT LEAVES

1 TSP SUGAR

PROSECCO, TO TOP

MINT, TO GARNISH

Add the cognac, sugar and mint leaves to a highball glass filled with crushed ice and churn.

Top with chilled Prosecco and more crushed ice and garnish with mint sprigs.

105

SBAGLIATO

1 MEASURE CAMPARI

1 MEASURE SWEET VERMOUTH

2 MEASURES PROSECCO

ORANGE, TO GARNISH

Add the ingredients to a rocks glass filled with cubed ice, stir briefly and garnish with a slice of orange.

ROSSINI

4 STRAWBERRIES

1 TSP SUGAR SYRUP

PROSECCO, TO TOP

Add the strawberries and sugar syrup to a blender or food processor and blend until smooth.

Pour into a Champagne flute and top with chilled Prosecco.

FRENCH 75

1 MEASURE GIN

½ MEASURE LEMON JUICE

½ MEASURE SUGAR SYRUP

PROSECCO, TO TOP

LEMON, TO GARNISH

Shake the gin, lemon juice and sugar syrup vigorously and strain into a Champagne flute.

Top with chilled Prosecco and garnish with a lemon twist.

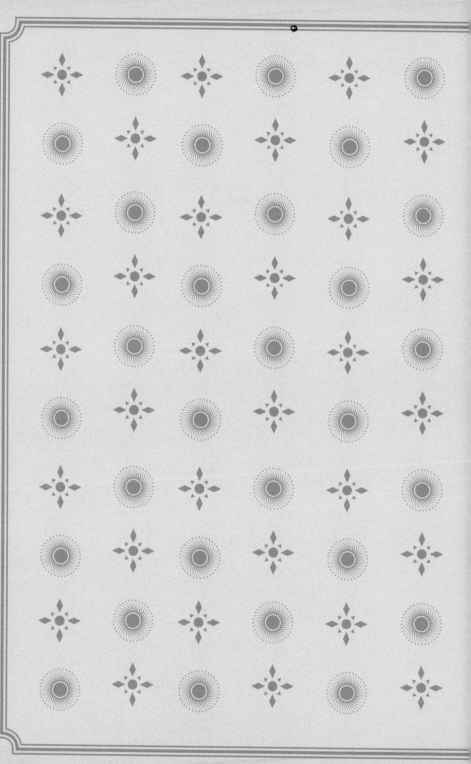

TIPS & TECHNIQUES FOR CRAFTING THE PERFECT COCKTAIL

WHAT MAKES A GOOD COCKTAIL?

Good cocktails, like good food, are based around quality ingredients. As with cooking, using fresh and homemade ingredients can often make a huge difference between a good drink and an outstanding drink. All of this can be found in department stores, online or in kitchen shops.

COCKTAIL INGREDIENTS

ICE This is a key part of cocktails and you'll need lots of it. Purchase it from your supermarket or freeze big tubs of water, then crack this up to use in your drinks. If you're hosting a big party and want to serve some punches, which will need lots of ice, it may be worthwhile finding if you have a local ice supplier that supplies catering companies, as this can be much more cost effective.

CITRUS JUICE It's important to use fresh citrus juice in your drinks; bottled versions taste awful and will not produce good drinks. Store your fruit out of the refrigerator at room temperature. Look for a soft-skinned fruit for juicing, which you can do with a juicer or citrus press. You can keep fresh citrus juice for a couple of days in the refrigerator, sealed to prevent oxidation.

SUGAR SYRUP You can buy sugar syrup or you can make your own. The most basic form of sugar syrup is made by mixing caster sugar and hot water together, and stirring until the sugar has dissolved. The key when preparing sugar syrups is to use a 1:1 ratio of sugar to liquid. White sugar acts as a flavour enhancer, while dark sugars have unique, more toffee flavours and work well with dark spirits.

BASIC SUGAR SYRUP RECIPE
Makes 1 litre (1¾ pints) of sugar syrup.
Dissolve 1 kg (2 lb) caster sugar in 1 litre (1¾ pints) of hot water.
Allow to cool.
Sugar syrup will keep in a sterilized bottle stored in the refrigerator for up to 2 weeks.

CINNAMON-INFUSED COGNAC
Add 2 cinnamon sticks to 500ml (17 fl oz) Cognac and leave to infuse for 2–3 days.

CHOOSING GLASSWARE

There are many different cocktails, but they all fall into one of three categories: long, short or shot. Long drinks generally have more mixer than alcohol, often served with ice and a straw. The terms 'straight up' and 'on the rocks' are synonymous with the short drink, which tends to be more about the spirit, often combined with a single mixer at most. Finally, there is the shot which is made up mainly from spirits and liqueurs, designed to give a quick hit of alcohol. Glasses are tailored to the type of drinks they will contain.

CHAMPAGNE FLUTE   Used for Champagne or Champagne cocktails, the narrow mouth of the flute helps the drink to stay fizzy.

CHAMPAGNE SAUCER   A classic glass, but not very practical for serving Champagne as the drink quickly loses its fizz.

MARGARITA OR COUPETTE GLASS   When used for a Margarita, the rim is dipped in salt. Also used for daiquiris and other fruit-based cocktails.

HIGHBALL GLASS   Suitable for any long cocktail, such as a Long Island Iced Tea.

COLLINS GLASS This is similar to a highball glass but is slightly narrower.

WINE GLASS Sangria is often served in one, but they are not usually used for cocktails.

OLD-FASHIONED GLASS Also known as a rocks glass, this is great for any drink that's served on the rocks or straight up.

SHOT GLASS Often found in two sizes — for a single or double measure. They are ideal for a single mouthful.

BALLOON GLASS Often used for fine spirits. The glass can be warmed to encourage the release of the drink's aroma.

HURRICANE GLASS Mostly found in beach bars, used for creamy, rum-based drinks.

BOSTON GLASS Often used by bartenders for mixing cocktails, good for fruity drinks.

TODDY GLASS A toddy glass is generally used for a hot drink, such as Irish Coffee.

SLING GLASS This has a very short stemmed base and is most famously used for a Singapore Sling.

MARTINI GLASS Also known as a cocktail glass, its thin neck design makes sure your hand can't warm the glass, or the cocktail.

USEFUL EQUIPMENT

Some pieces of equipment, such as shakers and the correct glasses, are vital for any cocktail party, while others, like ice buckets, can be obtained at a later date if needed. Below is a wishlist for anyone who wants to make cocktails on a regular basis.

SHAKER The Boston shaker is the most simple option, but it needs to be used in conjunction with a hawthorne strainer. Alternatively you could choose a shaker with a built-in strainer.

MEASURE OR JIGGER Single and double measures are available and are essential when you are mixing ingredients so that the proportions are always the same. One measure is 25 ml or 1 fl oz.

MIXING GLASS A mixing glass is used for those drinks that require only a gentle stirring before they are poured or strained.

HAWTHORNE STRAINER This type of strainer is often used in conjunction with a Boston shaker, but a simple tea strainer will also work well.

BAR SPOON Similar to a teaspoon but with a long handle, a bar spoon is used for stirring, layering and muddling drinks.

MUDDLING STICK Similar to a pestle, which will work just as well, a muddling stick, or muddler, is used to crush fruit or herbs in a glass or shaker for drinks like the Mojito.

BOTTLE OPENER Choose a bottle opener with two attachments, one for metal-topped bottles and a corkscrew for wine bottles.

POURERS A pourer is inserted into the top of a spirit bottle to enable the spirit to flow in a controlled manner.

FOOD PROCESSOR A food processor or blender is useful for making frozen cocktails and smoothies.

EQUIPMENT FOR GARNISHING Many drinks are garnished with fruit on cocktail sticks and these are available in wood, plastic or glass. Exotic drinks may be prettified with a paper umbrella and several long drinks are served with straws or swizzle sticks.

TECHNIQUES

With just a few basic techniques, your bartending skills will be complete. Follow the instructions to hone your craft.

BLENDING Frozen cocktails and smoothies are blended with ice in a blender until they are of a smooth consistency. Be careful not to add too much ice as this will dilute the cocktail. It's best to add a little at a time.

SHAKING The best-known cocktail technique and probably the most common. Used to mix ingredients thoroughly and quickly, and to chill the drink before serving.
1 Half-fill a cocktail shaker with ice cubes, or cracked or crushed ice.
2 If the recipe calls for a chilled glass add a few ice cubes and some cold water to the glass, swirl it around and discard.
3 Add the ingredients to the shaker and shake until a frost forms on the outside.
4 Strain the cocktail into the glass and serve.

MUDDLING A technique used to bring out the flavours of herbs and fruit using a blunt tool called a muddler.
1 Add chosen herb(s) to a highball glass. Add some sugar syrup and some lime wedges.
2 Hold the glass firmly and use a muddler or pestle to twist and press down.

3 Continue for 30 seconds, top up with crushed ice and add remaining ingredients.

DOUBLE-STRAINING   To prevent all traces of puréed fruit and ice fragments from entering the glass, use a shaker with a built-in strainer in conjunction with a hawthorne strainer. A fine strainer also works well.

LAYERING   Some spirits can be served layered on top of each other, causing 'lighter' spirits to float on top of your cocktail.
1 Pour the first ingredient into a glass, taking care that it does not touch the sides.
2 Position a bar spoon in the centre of the glass, rounded part down and facing you. Rest the spoon against the side of the glass as your pour the second ingredient down the spoon. It should float on top of the first liquid.
3 Repeat with the third ingredient, then carefully remove the spoon.

STIRRING   Used when the ingredients need to be mixed and chilled, but also maintain their clarity. This ensures there are no ice fragments or air bubbles throughout the drink. Some cocktails require the ingredients to be prepared in a mixing glass, then strained into the serving glass.
1 Add ingredients to a glass, in recipe order.
2 Use a bar spoon to stir the drink, lightly or vigorously, as described in the recipe.
3 Finish the drink with any decoration and serve.

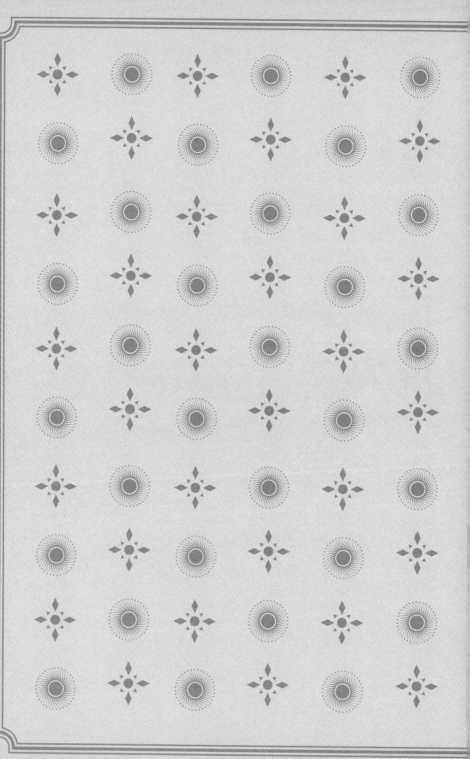

INDEX

PICTURE CREDITS